BRITAIN'S ♜ HERITAGE

Landscape Gardens

Sarah Rutherford

AMBERLEY

Chatsworth House and bridge. (Chatsworth House Trust)

Cover: Chatsworth Park, designed by Lancelot 'Capability' Brown in the 1760s. (Chatsworth House Trust)

First published 2017

Amberley Publishing
The Hill, Stroud
Gloucestershire, GL5 4EP

www.amberley-books.com

Copyright © Sarah Rutherford, 2017

The right of Sarah Rutherford to be identified
as the Author of this work has been asserted
in accordance with the Copyrights, Designs and
Patents Act 1988.

ISBN 978 1 4456 6993 9 (paperback)
ISBN 978 1 4456 6994 4 (ebook)

British Library Cataloguing in Publication Data.
A catalogue record for this book is available from
the British Library.

Printed in the UK.

Contents

1

Introduction: Britain's Quiet Revolution

The landscape garden: Britain's own artistic and horticultural revolution. This quiet revolt against the formal garden styles of Europe germinated and grew in Georgian Britain and Ireland in the eighteenth century. It blossomed in thousands of unique and sinuous works of art symbolising the creative spirit of the times. The landscape garden is a garden in the broadest sense: ornamental and natural-looking, on a large scale around a country house, including a park and pleasure grounds, with views into the countryside beyond. This startling break-out from the formal gardens of the Italian Renaissance, Holland and France burst into our very own national style, naturalistic and wide-spreading, embracing the wavy line and swelling hill in a riot of inspirational vision. From the 1750s it spread across Britain and Ireland and was embraced worldwide as its popularity continued into the next century. This landscape style is justly celebrated as the most important contribution Britain has made to the visual arts.

All this native beauty and success relied mainly on a simple palette of elements, used inspirationally: water, grass and trees. These had endless permutations depending on the place and its own features. It looked natural, but was to a large degree artificial, from the hand of man. The subject was the many country house estates owned by the wealthy and powerful. The landscape garden flowed around the country house with ornamental pleasure grounds seamlessly set in bucolic parkland, usually focused on a lake and planted with

The landscape garden is justly celebrated as the most important British contribution to the visual arts worldwide. Blenheim Palace, Oxfordshire, is one of the best, by 'Capability' Brown. (S. Rutherford)

specimen trees and clumps, the pasture grazed by agricultural livestock and horses. The walled kitchen garden, remaining uncompromisingly geometric in shape and layout, was often banished far out in the park along with the flower garden. Everything was linked by drives and walks and long views were flung out into the surrounding countryside.

Germinating in the 1700s and 1710s, growing on from the 1720s to the 1740s, and flowering from the 1750s, this landscape style quickly swept away the straight lines and rigidity of past generations. As well as being tranquil and attractive, it reduced costs, replacing gardeners with sheep or cattle to keep down large expanses of grass, although later on the formal flower garden began to make a comeback. The style became ubiquitous in Britain and Ireland and perhaps 4,000 or 5,000 landscape gardens were created.

Did you know?

The Formal French Garden Style
French garden style boomed in Britain between the Restoration of Charles II in 1660, when he returned from Sun King Louis XIV's royal court, until the 1720s. *Parterres de broderie* had swirling Baroque designs of beds picked out in flowers or patterns of coloured fine minerals or grass, fountains played in round or rectangular stone basins, formal canals and avenues of trees framed axles from the mansion into the wider landscape, with serried groves of trees in grid pattern and formal wildernesses of trees and shrubs. Fruit trees were trained on any available wall. Sculpture and ornamental ironwork burgeoned.

Versailles, the vast palace and geometric gardens of power. With this display the French Sun King, Louis XIV, impressed the whole of Europe in the seventeenth century. Pierre Patel, 1668. (Bridgeman Images)

By the 1720s most British gardens had little original about them. Corseted in the geometric lines of European models, they aimed to copy places such as the dazzling palace gardens of Sun King Louis XIV's France. This garden fashion was led from the 1660s by our Stuart kings Charles II and James II, who had lived at King Louis' court after the Civil War, before the Restoration of the monarchy, and then in the 1690s and 1700s by Dutch King William III and Queen Mary. Gardens were strictly controlled, on a regular layout of straight lines. Great avenues strode out from country houses beyond rectangular forecourts and gardens into the wider rural landscape. These were, however, based on models such as Versailles, which made the most of dead flat French landscapes. They were not really suited to Britain's countryside as the effect of endless straight vistas was wrecked by the hills that inevitably got in the way.

Did you know?

French Designers in England
Louis XIV's gardener Le Notre, hugely celebrated in France, is linked in England with Hampton Court. His associate André Mollet came to England and advised on the French style in the 1660s. John Rose (1629–77) trained under le Notre and became the finest practical gardener in England in the 1660s and 1670s. Rose reproduced le Notre's favourite features with parterres, courts enclosed by high clipped hedges, allees and vistas.

The gardens of Hampton Court Palace, west of London, were influenced by the geometry and scale of Versailles, including the canal and Fountain Court that still survive, although in simplified form. Leonard Knyff, *c.* 1702. (Royal Collection Trust © Her Majesty Queen Elizabeth II, 2017/Bridgeman Images)

Above: One of myriad geometric gardens surrounding the palace at Versailles, with fountains, pools, sculpture and ornamental ironwork, within clipped hedges. This was the place to party! (Yale Center for British Art, Paul Mellon Collection)

Below: British gardens copied the French style with geometric compartments and parterres of plants, raked sand and gravel. Denham Place, Buckinghamshire, c. 1695. (Yale Center for British Art, Paul Mellon Collection)

From 1720 the muscular, Frenchified force of geometry gave way in British gardens to the more natural Serpentine Line of Beauty that Hogarth satirised in the 1750s. This naturalistic form, taken up ubiquitously in the country estate, became the new British symbol of wealth, power and status, contrasting with the severe boxiness of the contemporary Palladian and neo-classical mansions it surrounded.

The landscape garden is far more than just the ornamental setting for a country house, it is instead the outdoor equivalent of paintings displayed indoors on the walls. It is complex and diverse, embracing estate management on a large decorative scale, encompassing agriculture, architecture, sporting features, water features and fishing, timber production, as well as the essential horticulture, both productive and ornamental. This work of art is not just decorative but an economic unit, and highly functional too, with features to amuse, and for sport, all clothed in a variety of plants to screen and frame views and make the most of the land form.

Why was the landscape style suited to succeed so brilliantly in Britain and Ireland at this time? The circumstances were just right for it to flourish by the 1750s in several ways. The threat of civil war receded after the Jacobite Rising of 1745–46, peace reigned at home, and great wealth was to be had by some from trading with the colonies, including the products of slavery. Political stability broke out and financial policy (including the founding of the Bank of England), along with global expansion, allowed investment in manufacturing. The impending Industrial Revolution benefitted many park-making owners financially.

In the British landscape garden the serpentine line of beauty broke out of the corset of European geometry from the 1720s. Hogarth satirised it in his *Analysis of Beauty* (1753). (S. Rutherford)

Transport improved greatly. Landowners could reach their estates from London more easily and quickly with improvements in roads, carriage technology and horse breeding. Key technologies of the time, including agriculture, land drainage, water technology and civil engineering, were developing fast and were essential to the landscaper. Engineering in these gardens was of great significance, predating what are generally regarded as pioneering advances of the Industrial Revolution and the Canal Age (1763–90). Economically, the amount of money spent landscaping estates formed a major part of the national economy, with 'Capability' Brown's contribution probably the most significant. His innate business sense underpinned his extensive contributions to this financial and landscaping frenzy.

The countryside at last became a civilised concept to be shown off as land ownership changed and great swathes became more freely available for creative (and wealthy) owners. Previously owners had difficulty uniting tracts of land large enough for parks because of archaic property rights, with many small owners having strips of land scattered across medieval 'open field' systems. Georgian owners could now use parliamentary Enclosure Acts to acquire and unlock vast areas of land ideal for creative landscaping with trees, grass and water in a single vision. This also set the scene for the Agricultural Revolution. Improvements in land management were embraced in these newly united tracts of land, turning them into a new breed of ornamental parks in which a display of productivity was important.

Improvements in transport, including horses, carriages and roads, gave owners easier access to their country estates to enjoy civilised and social life there with their social circle. Thoroughbreds beautified and grazed the new parks. The racehorse Pumpkin by Stubbs, 1774. (Yale Center for British Art, Paul Mellon Collection)

By sprinkling trees in parks owners proclaimed that they were wealthy enough not to need these great areas for profitable arable crops, as it was difficult to plough around scattered trees. Instead they could maintain their prestigious new parks as pasture by grazing with the latest thoroughbred horses, a highly bred status symbol, and improved breeds of livestock, which displayed their grasp of advancing agricultural husbandry. Enclosure and wealth allowed owners to move villages that were untidy and inconveniently intruded into their Arcadian views, and rebuild them out of sight, such as Nuneham Courtenay near Oxford and Milton Abbas in Dorset. Sporting activities were built into the design, particularly hunting, shooting and fishing, which were also advancing in their methods and technologies.

So the scene was ripe for spectacular changes in Georgian parks and gardens.

The landscape style was epitomised by genius landscaper Lancelot 'Capability' Brown (1716–83), the Shakespeare of gardening. Brown worked throughout England and Wales, his greatest works at places such as Blenheim Palace, Oxfordshire; Alnwick Castle, Northumberland; Chatsworth, Derbyshire; and Petworth House, Sussex. Plenty of competent landscape designers worked in this style, such as Thomas White (1739–1811), Richard Woods (c. 1716–93) and William Emes (1730–1803), but they were generally regionally based and worked for fewer grand clients. The style hybridised into the next generation, in the inevitable reaction, when Brown's self-styled successor Humphry Repton (1752–1818) took the concept into the next century, bringing back the flower garden near the house. An offshoot was the Picturesque and Sublime: closely related but more rugged versions of the park and pleasure ground. These designers advised owners who were keen to follow the new and relaxed fashion. By 1800 Europe was gripped by landscape garden fever, which was known by the French as the Anglo-Chinoise style. Wealthy owners enthusiastically landscaped continental gardens, adapting the British style as far away as Russia.

2

The Beginning of the End of Formal Gardens, 1710s–20s

The landscape garden sprang up in Britain around the time when a new ruling house took the throne, and vast wealth and access to land ownership was becoming available to the lucky few. The taste of the elite in showing off new possessions and estates was a major factor in the Hanoverian politics of power and wealth. In the 1710s a genteel British revolution against the geometric European style in gardens began, just as the Hanoverian King George I arrived from Germany and took up the throne in a peaceful and civilised manner in 1714. The four Kings George escorted and embraced the British landscape movement as it flourished through more than a century, until the death of George IV in 1830.

The garden at Llanerch, Denbighshire, new in 1662, reflected the Italian Renaissance style, which in turn influenced French gardens. Intimate compartments were connected with the house, in the manner of the sixteenth-century Villa Lante near Rome. (Yale Center for British Art, Paul Mellon Collection)

Did you know?

Garden-Designing Duo London & Wise

George London (*c.* 1640–1714) and Henry Wise (1653–1738) were the most prestigious and prolific garden designers between the 1690s and 1710s. They embodied an unbeatable blend of English practicality and imagination and were contemporaries of one of the greatest English composers, Henry Purcell, and of court painter Sir Godfrey Kneller. In 1681 London, with John Rose, founded a nursery at Brompton Park, west of London, and around 1688 took Wise into partnership. The nursery supplied plants for their new schemes. They worked for King William III at Hampton Court and Kensington Palace, and at many aristocrats' seats including Chatsworth, Melbourne Hall, Castle Howard and Blenheim. Wise was royal gardener to Queen Anne and then after 1714 to George I. The pair were the last of the great English formalists. Most of their work went to make way for the new landscape style.

This peaceful home-grown revolt against European landscape design was spearheaded by intellectuals and style gurus in their writings. A few brilliant and articulate men wielded great influence in this arena. From the 1700s and 1710s a campaign against the rigidly formal gardens took hold and by 1730 was unstoppable. Lords Shaftesbury and Burlington, who were owners and amateur designers, architect Sir John Vanbrugh and writers Joseph Addison and Alexander Pope fronted the new landscape movement. Their strong steer led to one of the artistic triumphs of British history.

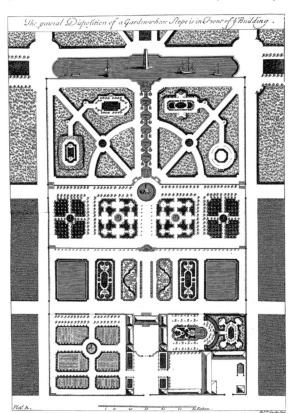

These arbiters of taste judged that in the formal style all contact with nature in gardens had gone. They decreed that it had to be re-established and extended into the wider landscape. Literary lions Joseph Addison, Richard Steel and Alexander Pope published the earliest, vehement criticism and suggested how things could be more naturalistic. Addison disliked the Italian gardens he had recently

This French plan was published for the British audience to copy or adapt in 1712 in *The Theory and Practice of Gardening* (John James).

Above: The Privy Garden, Hampton Court, framed Christopher Wren's contemporary palace façade for the Dutch King William III and his English wife Queen Mary. Garden and building combine as a perfect work of orderly, outdoor art. (Charles Micklewright)

Below: Hedges were trained like architectural features, copying Versailles. Hartwell House, Buckinghamshire, Balthasar Nebot, 1730s. (Bucks County Museum)

visited, and urged his British readers to discard garden formality and abolish parterres, clipped topiary and hedges and avenues. He exhorted them, instead, to embrace informal and naturalistic principles, also including a profitable purpose. He sketched a dream world, principally an Arcadia of natural scenery, ruled over by the Goddess of Liberty, supported by two other goddesses, Plenty and Commerce. The zeitgeist dictated freedom from unnecessary constraints (at least for the wealthy and powerful). This creed struck home and movers and shakers of the day enthusiastically embraced it in their landscaping activities.

Pope was still more fiercely critical and from 1713, starting in an essay in the *Guardian*, he continued to promote the virtues of nature and asymmetry in witty verse and prose. He was also a great gardener, his brilliance widely recognised, and so he not only made his own famous garden at his villa in Twickenham but advised widely in fashionable and political society. Groves, wildernesses, dells, grottoes and winding paths started to break out of the stifling grids into more agreeable serpentine lines, but still axial walks, vistas and quincunxes of trees sliced across and confined these new lines in the old geometry, as at Lord Burlington's influential Chiswick House, Middlesex.

The designers weighed in to support the writers. In 1715 Stephen Switzer in *The Nobleman, Gentleman and Gardener's Recreation* announced the beginning of the end of Formal Gardening. He believed that all art was based on the study of nature. A garden should embrace the distant prospect of nature beyond it. By 1726 the momentum was strong and not to be turned back. Batty Langley raged in his *New Principles of Gardening* against gardens 'so crowded with evergreens so that they had more of the aspect of a nursery than

Seemingly endless avenues were ideal for the flat French countryside. Sometimes they worked well in England too. At fairly flat Wimpole, Cambridgeshire, Charles Bridgeman planted massive elm avenues including the 2½-mile-long south avenue. Knyff and Kip, *c.* 1708. (S. Rutherford)

a Garden of Pleasure ... always stuffed up with trifling flower knots, Parterres or cut-work, Embroidery, Wilderness of Evergreens'. The death knell sounded, he continued, 'Nor is there any thing more shocking than a stiff, formal regular Garden.' The green revolution was in train. It just required limitless imagination and a deep pocket to join in the shock of the new.

Their idea of abolishing rigid geometry in gardens was being seriously explored by a few inquisitive and innovative owners and great designers in the 1720s, leading the way to a more relaxed garden style. Although these early gardens were highly influential in steering others, initially there was no great rush by owners. Many people stuck with the conventional layouts for decades, not least because it was much easier to continue with a smaller garden in the formal manner than try and make it into a mini-Blenheim parkland.

In this early phase of change, gardens were still enclosed and divided by straight boundaries, but intricate parterres of flowers, hedges and topiary started to give way to the wilderness shrubbery with paths wriggling between the shrubs and trees in a very contrived manner. Switzer and Langley showed plans with tightly curved paths through compartments, or 'cabinets' of woodwork, drawn from earlier French models, but these were closely confined and still obviously displayed the hand of man. These sorts of lines were used in gardens by designers including Charles Bridgeman and were gleefully taken up in the offshoot Rococo style of the 1730s–60s, which was still more contrived. But it was a breakaway movement from the European lines and heralded still greater changes.

Practically, the swelling contours of the rolling British and Irish countryside were much better suited to something based on naturalistic curves, and could more easily be adapted to these, rather than struggling with the rigid avenues of France, which suited the terrain there as the countryside was mostly unrelievedly flat.

Topiary and Evergreens

Formal gardens used evergreens to frame the strict lines and banish the desolation of winter with perpetual foliage. Yew was a good subject as it grew relatively fast, but box, Portugal laurel and tender myrtle and bay were also popular. These were clipped not just into hedges dividing garden 'rooms', but also worked up into specimens in geometric shapes such as cones, globes and pyramids and into fanciful figures of birds, animals or objects. Their very complexity was mocked in the 1710s as the ridiculous zenith of the formal garden, and then they began to go out of fashion. The satirist Alexander Pope made up a spoof nursery catalogue of topiary specimens for sale in 1713, including:

> Adam and Eve in yew, Adam a little shattered by the fall of the Tree of Knowledge in the great storm: Eve and the serpent very flourishing ...
> St George in box: his arm scarce long enough but will be condition to stick the dragon by next April.
> Divers modern poets in bays, somewhat blighted, to be disposed of, a pennyworth.
> A quickset hog, shot up into a porcupine, by being forgot a week in rainy weather ...
> Noah's ark in holly, standing on the mount, the ribs a little damaged for want of water.

Levens Hall, Cumbria, still boasts a great collection of clipped specimens.

Formal landscapes were gradually reworked into the coming style in a trickle that became a gush by the 1740s. Stowe in Buckinghamshire was in the vanguard. When initially designed by Bridgeman in the 1710s–20s using straight lines, the garden was daringly not strictly symmetrical. The newly introduced ha-ha enclosed it, so that the sunken boundary wall allowed uninterrupted views of the surrounding countryside with its swelling hills and

The delicacy of individual flowers was much valued in formal gardens, here displayed to great effect in a sunken parterre, adorned with much topiary and sculpture. As usual, fruit trees were trained all over the walls. Pierrepont House, Nottingham, 1690s. (Yale Center for British Art, Paul Mellon Collection)

bucolic farmland. Wiggly paths crept in. The garden was adorned with many buildings, some modest and retiring such as St Augustine's Cave; others were substantial and innovative such as Vanbrugh's Rotondo, the first of myriad circular-domed 'temples' perched precariously on columns that were sprinkled across gardens for the rest of the century. The native landscape started to dictate the layout to take advantage of the 'genius of the place'.

Pope in his *Epistle to Lord Burlington* (1731) summed up the painterly quality of the new kind of garden and how it responded to the spirit of the place:

Consult the genius of the place in all;
That tells the waters or to rise, or fall;
Or helps th' ambitious hill the heav'ns to scale,
Or scoops in circling theatres the vale;

Did you know?

Designer Charles Bridgeman (d. 1738)

In the 1720s–30s Bridgeman spanned the formality of London and Wise's French-style designs and the truly naturalistic landscape garden of 'Capability' Brown and his contemporaries. Within formal design lines he started to soften the layout. He 'borrowed' views of the scenery beyond the garden by using the ha-ha, a sunken wall invisible from the garden that prevented stock invading and made the country beyond the park part of the scene. Major commissions included Stowe, Buckinghamshire; Wimpole, Cambridgeshire; Blenheim Palace, Oxfordshire; Claremont, Surrey, but much was lost to later landscape fashion.

From 1720 Kent, Bridgeman and their successors presided over the mass destruction of our formal gardens on a scale unmatched in Europe. In Britain little survives to compare with the great Italian villas such as the Renaissance Villa d'Este near Rome. (S. Rutherford)

> Calls in the country, catches opening glades,
> Joins willing woods, and varies shades from shades,
> Now breaks, or now directs, th' intending lines;
> Paints as you plant, and, as you work, designs.'

The existing formal gardens complemented the symmetry/geometry of the country houses in Baroque and Palladian style and their loss has had its critics. It has been said that Kent, Bridgeman and their successors from 1720 onwards were responsible for the mass destruction on a scale unmatched in any other European country of the numerous old formal gardens, leaving intact few great British and Irish equivalents to the Italian Boboli Gardens and Villas d'Este and Lante, the French palaces of Versailles and Vaux le Vicomte, or Heilbronn in Austria. They swept away great works of landscape art just because they were based on straight lines and circles – huge canals, viewing mounts, parterres, avenues, hedges, statues. It was lucky that Hampton Court survived, but only because the king lived elsewhere and had no interest in changing it.

Did you know?

The Best Early Gardens to Visit
The best formal gardens include Powis Castle, Powys; Levens Hall, Cumbria; Westbury Court, Gloucestershire; Hampton Court, Middlesex; Melbourne Hall, Derbyshire; Cliveden, Bucks; Castle Howard, North Yorkshire.

3
William Kent: Nature Makes a Comeback, 1730s–40s

Nature was getting the upper hand in gardens by the 1730s, with still more relaxed serpentine lines guiding the arrangement of water, grass and planting. Writer and style guru Horace Walpole, later in the century, proclaimed this to be the genesis of the British national garden style. Frenchified gardens were vanquished!

The Grand Tour of Europe had a profound effect on Georgian garden owners and designers. In the name of education wealthy young men of good family spent an extended time, sometimes several years, touring Europe, mainly in Italy and other Mediterranean countries previously colonised by classical cultures. Their education at home had revolved

Arcadian paintings by Claude Lorrain inspired wealthy British Grand Tourists to evoke similar scenes in their gardens. Chiswick House, Middlesex, and Stourhead, Wiltshire were obviously influenced. *Landscape with Aeneas at Delos*, 1672. (Bridgeman Images)

around the Antique classical authors and they could easily relate to the remains and related culture they found. The young, rich Georgians returned to Britain full of enthusiasm for the past, experiences and artistic trophies to display. They were keen to evoke in their own grounds peaceful and swelling Arcadian scenes painted by Claude and Poussin, and the rougher and wild landscapes of Salvator Rosa, as well as the pastoral Roman poetry of Virgil.

Designer William Kent and his patron Lord Burlington visited Italy and came back inspired by the classical buildings and countryside. They were besotted by Italy and used it to enrich their work. They set to, to transform the landscape of Chiswick House near London with the architecture derived from Palladio's genius of the sixteenth century, set within the landscapes of ancient Italy, and allusions to the Latin pastoral poets, particularly Virgil. Together, and extraordinarily, this unlikely pair influenced the shaping of English gardens at this crucial time in their development.

Did you know?

Yorkshire Designer and Artist William Kent (1685–1748)
Kent was the father of the naturalistic landscape style in the 1730s–40s, softening garden lines further. A not very good painter from Bridlington who trained in Italy, he became a talented designer of buildings, gardens and stage scenery, with a sense of humour. He was a contemporary of composer George Frideric Handel and artist William Hogarth. His master works include Chiswick House, Greater London; the Elysian Fields at Stowe, Buckinghamshire; Claremont Landscape Garden, Surrey, and Rousham, Oxfordshire.

At Chiswick House in the 1720s–30s, Lord Burlington and Kent, on their return from Italy, made a trailblazing garden around a new Italianate villa. (Chiswick House & Gardens, photo by Clive Boursnell)

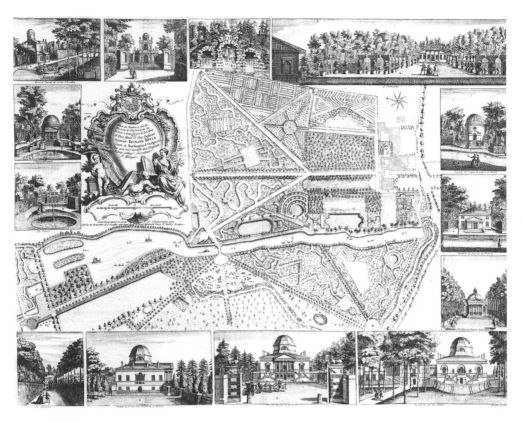

Above: In a phase between the strictly formal and the relaxed lines of the landscape garden, Chiswick House overflowed with convoluted paths and had a serpentine 'river'. Order was preserved as they were corsetted within a framework of straight avenues. Map by John Roque, 1736. (Bridgeman Images)

Left: William Kent (1685–1748), the godfather of naturalistic landscape garden designers. He banished straight lines in the Elysian Fields at Stowe and at Rousham, encouraging other garden-makers to try out the new relaxed style and be innovative themselves. (Bridgeman Images)

The Elysian Fields, Stowe, a sinuous work of art William Kent created from scratch for Lord Cobham in the 1730s that banishes the straight line. (Yale Center for British Art, Paul Mellon Collection)

In the new garden style the influence of Italian landscape crept in when the composition began to be seen with a painterly eye. In particular it was seen through the eyes of favoured painters who chose the gentler parts of the Italian countryside, including the Roman Campagna, and bathed by them in a gorgeous Arcadian glow. These French landscape painters of the previous century painted Arcadian scenes, often as the setting for Biblical or classical tableaux, but in each the countryside was the star, with classical temples, columns and ruins framed by rivers, seas and beautiful skies. Claude and Poussin painted serene scenes while those by Salvator Rosa were more dramatic.

Alongside the landscapes of ancient Italy the flood of rich British visitors on the Grand Tour took up antique architecture and its interpretation by the great Renaissance architect Palladio around Venice as their most favoured style for houses and garden buildings in the world of these new gardens. Burlington's new Chiswick House was based on a Palladian country house – the Villa Rotondo, Vicenza, near Venice. It formed the most important building in his new garden design with Kent.

Kent worked on the most important gardens that were trail-blazers for the landscape garden: at Claremont, Holkham, Chiswick, Kensington Palace, and was often reworking Bridgeman's gardens. Rousham and the Elysian Fields at Stowe are masterpieces which survive well, the one remodelling Bridgeman's framework of a few years earlier, the other laid out anew on the blank canvas of a lost village valley. In these two, as at Chiswick, he made the most of relatively small spaces, idealising the Italian countryside in an English rural setting, using winding walks, pools and rivers, trees to separate the various areas and surprise when they were revealed, and the interplay of light and shade. Each was populated with statues

Above: Venus Vale, Rousham, Oxfordshire, drawing by William Kent, 1730s. It is one of Kent's most influential schemes, within a more formal Bridgeman design. It still overlooks the meandering River Cherwell, 'calling in' the Arcadian countryside beyond. (Mr & Mrs C. Cottrell-Dormer)

Below: Kent designed park scenery, including at Holkham and Euston in East Anglia. Trees framed his buildings (here a deer house) like naturalistic theatre scenery, both as a backcloth, and with flanking clumps like theatrical flats to alter perspective. (Yale Center for British Art, Paul Mellon Collection)

of classical gods, heroes and writers and framed a plethora of Claudean buildings to evoke Italy in the Roman Augustan age but set firmly in the British countryside. Kent also worked on a larger, parkland scale, seen at Holkham Hall, Norfolk, and Euston Park in Suffolk, leaving behind him quirky sketches of his vision and the people he imagined using these Arcadian landscapes.

Did you know?

The *Ferme Orné*
Woburn Farm, Surrey, and the Leasowes, West Midlands, were *fermes ornés*, or ornamented farms, designed by their owners and fashionable from the 1720s to the 1760s. Rural paddocks were surrounded by floral walks planted with colourful shrubs, trees and hedges, from which to admire the agricultural land and livestock.

Not everything was classical in the new regime. The native medieval Gothic building style re-appeared with dramatic mock churches and fortifications built prominently on hillsides. Stowe had early Gothic buildings as park eye-catchers, in the Bourbon Tower and Stowe Castle by architect James Gibbs (*c*. 1740). Gentleman architect Sanderson Miller was developing a convincing version, with mock ruins as eye-catchers, in the 1740s. He built his own Gothic tower at Radway in Warwickshire and designed various apparently decayed fortifications, starting at nearby Hagley in Worcestershire, with another later at Wimpole as the centrepiece of a 'Capability' Brown park, distantly seen from the house. Horace Walpole was bitten by the romantic Gothic bug in the 1740s and spent the rest of his life building and tinkering with his little castle, Strawberry Hill near Twickenham, close to Pope's own grotto and garden (but after Pope had died in 1744). Walpole's landscape garden had a tiny Gothic Chapel in the Woods and a painted timber Shell Seat in the form of a scallop shell.

In his garden at Strawberry Hill Walpole leant towards the Rococo (from the French for rockwork or pebble work, and shell). This whimsical, feminine style proved to be a byway in the 1730s–60s, an offshoot of the more purposeful march towards the fully fledged and more muscular landscape style. This short-lived fancy was based on elegantly writhing lines, asymmetry and quirky design, generally set in only a few acres. It was closely related to what other people were creating, with Kent's designs such as at Rousham and the Elysian Fields at Stowe, showing how styles at the time often overlapped. The contemporary idea of Chinese style appeared in many Rococo buildings. The landscape painter Thomas Robins immortalised these ephemeral gardens in beguiling views surrounded by frames depicting trailing plants, flowers, boughs of trees, sea shells and birds. Painswick Rococo Garden, Gloucestershire, is delightfully restored in this fanciful style, so prettily depicted by Robins. On its compact hillside site many eccentric little buildings are linked by paths and groves. Rocks, fossils and shells often formed part of the garden design, or physically adorned grottoes or shell houses. Numerous grottoes survive, including at Stourhead, Wiltshire, Stowe, Buckinghamshire, and Goodwood, Sussex.

Above: Horace Walpole, the champion of the landscape garden, created his own in miniature around his Gothic villa, Strawberry Hill near Twickenham from the 1740s. (Strawberry Hill Trust)
Below: Rococo style: small, intimate spaces, elegantly planted, and imaginative garden buildings. The shell theme giving the style its name is lavished in the border of this view of Painswick Rococo Garden, Gloucestershire. Thomas Robins, 1748. (S. Rutherford)

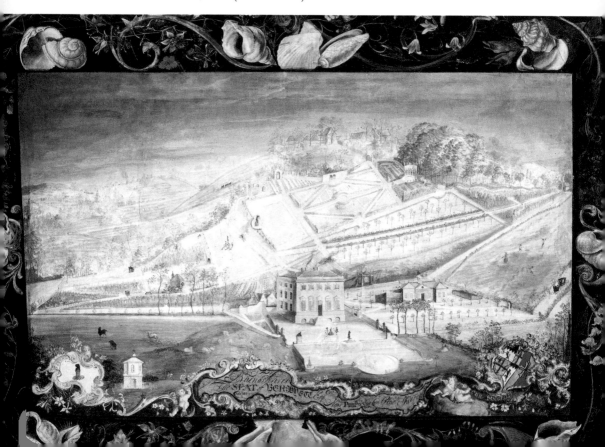

Above: Buildings at Painswick Rococo Garden are unique and whimsical, like the Gothic Eagle House. Like other garden buildings they close vistas and provide shelter and viewpoints in the route around the hilly garden. (Painswick Rococo Garden/Adrienn Bencsik)

Right: At Painshill, Surrey, owner Charles Hamilton made one of the best grottoes, the sparkling 'river' running through a labyrinth, reflected in the thousands of shards of mica crystals. (S. Rutherford)

4

The Landscape Garden: 1750 onwards

By 1750 the landscape garden came of age, after several overlapping stages of development, and it flourished into the next century. It was quickly embraced as the British landscape style and each is a work of art in its own right. It formed the large-scale ornamental grounds for what was usually a rather boxy country house. Strangely, it contrasted with the regularity of the architecture, as it had no evident orderliness of design, seeming to be purely natural. This belied the immense amount of art, planning and sheer hard work that lay behind it, and the intrinsic design relationship between the house and grounds.

Several standard elements harmonise in a landscape garden as the setting for the country house, in itself another work of art. Endlessly changing views of the landscape from the main rooms were essential, linking the house with its grounds. The best landscape gardens appear endless, though sometimes they only cover a few tens of acres, but if possible they take in a wider rural or marine landscape beyond the main design. They comprise pleasure grounds, a park sprinkled with specimen trees and clumps, snaky drives to the house, a large walled kitchen garden, enclosed by belts of sheltering woodland. If at all possible water is used as a lake or a 'river' (natural if possible, but artificial if necessary). The method of designing

The apparent simplicity of the landscape garden: water, grass and trees, in a world-class design by 'Capability' Brown, Blenheim Palace, Oxfordshire. The lake is 1½ miles long and covers 110 acres. (S. Rutherford)

Above: The landscape garden was the playground for wealthy families and social life in the country house estate. The Gwillym family at Atherton Hall; Arthur Devis, 1745–7. (Yale Center for British Art, Paul Mellon Collection)

Below: The landscape style looked as natural as possible, but emerged from much thought, artistic genius and hard work. Stourhead, Wiltshire, was designed by owner Henry Hoare over several decades from the 1740s. (National Trust Photographic Library/Jerry Harpur/Bridgeman Images)

these places was unique at the time, taking and enhancing the 'genius of the place', as it was labelled. In other words, using to the best effect the extent of land available, and the specific position, land form, climate, aspect, soil and other features united in a particular place.

The layout was to appear as natural as possible, although often existing trees were kept, even avenues – trees being highly valued for their timber – and enormous quantities of earth might be moved. The wider setting was essential to push views beyond the park boundary, to 'borrow' or 'call in' the interesting parts of the surrounding landscape that did not necessarily belong to the land owner but appeared as if it did. Existing structures with historic resonance, such as church towers and ruined castles, were good 'eye-catchers' that drew the eye along vistas beyond the park. If no suitable building existed to do this, new features were built on eminences. Thus sprouted myriad columns, obelisks, arches, artificial ruins, churches and towers in prominent places, just like stage scenery to fool the eye. With this extensive choice and a unique site every landscape garden was different.

Nature Transfigured by Art

The landscape garden actually became a better, idealised, version of the countryside. It emphasised the attractive aspects with clumps of trees dotted around swelling grazed slopes and hill tops, meandering lakes and rivers, enclosed by sheltering woodland. Uniquely at the time it reflected the existing land form, to make the best use of what was there already. Of course it was a very artificial construct, created sometimes with thousands of tons of earth moved, and villages too, and millions of trees planted. 'Capability' Brown described how he used the elements of his designs like punctuation: "'Now there' said he, pointing his finger, 'I make a comma, and there' pointing to another spot, 'where a more decided turn is

Did you know?

Lancelot 'Capability' Brown (1716–83)

Lancelot Brown was the foremost landscape designer of his day, advising from around 1750 until his death in early 1783 at over 250 places throughout England, with a few in Wales. He is the most important British landscape designer, the Face of the landscape

garden. His famous nickname came from his habit of advising prospective clients that their grounds, however unpromising, had 'great capabilities'. He was friends with the great actor and theatre manager David Garrick, and worked at the same time as Mozart and British artists Gainsborough, Reynolds and Stubbs. Masterpieces survive at Blenheim Palace, Oxfordshire; Petworth, Sussex; Wimpole Hall and Burghley, Cambridgeshire; Harewood, Yorkshire, and Alnwick Castle, Northumberland.

Lancelot 'Capability' Brown (1716-83), the greatest genius of the landscape garden: designer, architect, engineer, and businessman. His nickname came from his habit of advising owners that their grounds had 'capabilities' (i.e. potential). (Bridgeman Images)

Brown's first major position was at Stowe in the 1740s. Guided by owner Lord Cobham he swept away a formal French-style parterre and laid out lawns framed by trees. He became Royal Gardener to George III at Hampton Court in 1764. (Anna McEvoy)

proper, I make a colon; at another part, where an interruption is desirable to break the view, a parenthesis; now a full stop, and then I begin another subject.'" But it had a very relaxed feel to it and this was the point. Even so, these 'natural' landscapes were at odds with the architectural formality of the stately homes they embraced. Practically, the park coming up to the door of the house (e.g. at Petworth) meant it was difficult to keep the contents of the park floor out of the house and off the precious floor and its coverings.

Brown's obituary in 1783 summed up the desired effect of the landscape style: 'Such, however, was the effect of his genius that when he was the happiest man, he will be least remembered; so closely did he copy nature that his works will be mistaken.' The Georgian interpretation of nature's lines in this way, when viewed at the time, spoke of good husbandry, wealth, taste and power, as did the formal predecessors across the Channel, but more subtly than those. The open spaces contrasting grassy sward and sheets of water were as important as the built and planted areas in the proportions of the design.

This startling new style was especially suited to Britain and Ireland. It developed alongside the modernisation of land distribution and agriculture when Parliamentary Enclosures were at their height. In particular the growth of grass was highly prized and in this respect Britain and Ireland were the best in Europe. Their climate was perfectly suited to producing lush and nutritious grazing: as islands on the north-west edge of Europe they avoided the continental climate veering between devastating winter cold and scorching summer drought, helped by the Gulf Stream bringing relative warmth and blessed rain across the Atlantic. The new parks had many acres of sward sheltered by perimeter belts of trees, and scattered park trees filtering cooling and desiccating winds. All these created an ideal microclimate to encourage grass growth. For the same climatic reasons British and Irish garden lawns were known as the best in Europe too.

Above: As a freelance designer from 1750, Brown ran an extensive practice. His Chatsworth design was carried out in the 1760s by one of his many foremen, Michael Milliken, who he then took to Kew as the king's gardener there. (Chatsworth House Trust)

Below: Brown, in demand by the wealthy and powerful throughout his career, worked tirelessly until his sudden end in 1783, aged sixty-seven. Heveningham, Suffolk, is one of his last great works. (Yale Center for British Art, Paul Mellon Collection)

Modest landscape gardens might be only a few tens of acres in extent, but some were huge. Ickworth in Suffolk covers 1,800 acres; Stowe, Bucks, and Burghley, Cambridgeshire, 1,200 acres; Wimpole, also in Cambridgeshire, 500 acres, but Blenheim covers 2,400 acres. Lakes could be very large too. One of the greatest is Brown's at Blenheim, being 1½ miles long and 110 acres as a single sheet.

Landscape designers appeared from several walks of life. Whatever his background, the designer had to understand the natural land form, climate, water supply and soil conditions by visiting and seeing how they could all be manipulated to the best effect.

Many, like Brown, Richard Woods and William Emes, were working men with a broad range of practical skills and an eye for design who became professional designers. They often started as gardeners and turned landscapers, acquiring expertise in a wide range of subjects related to design and land management, including architecture, water engineering, surveying, land drainage, large-scale ground remodelling and forestry. They used competent foremen to execute the schemes, with teams of labourers on the ground, who sometimes set up on their own in various regions. This allowed the mastermind to juggle many sites at once, visiting occasionally to check up on progress. Brown had several dozen foremen, who struck out on their own, often with his blessing it seems, including Thomas White who was prolific in Scotland, Adam Mickle who began a dynasty of designers and Nathaniel Richmond who confined himself mainly to the Home Counties.

Architects too dabbled in landscape design, but not in the same quantities as the professionals' commissions. Sir William Chambers laid out the grounds for half of royal Kew Gardens, next to Brown's design for the other, riverside, half, building a monster 50-metre-high Chinese pagoda and Moorish Temple among other outlandish buildings for George III's mother, Princess Augusta. Robert Adam provided sinuous and attractive plans for Kedleston, Derbyshire, and possibly Osterley, Middlesex and other places. Plenty of other architects influenced these new landscapes.

Occasionally a wealthy owner had the flair, understanding and money to design his own country house landscape with the hand of genius. Outstanding examples were the banker

Landscape parks were productive as well as beautiful, needing livestock to keep them grazed. At Wimpole Park Brown built a Gothic ruin in the 1760s as an eye-catcher in the pasture. (National Trust Photographic Library/Justin Minns/Bridgeman Images)

Above: Architects sometimes designed landscape gardens as well as landscape designers and owners. William Chambers designed one half of the present Kew Gardens for Princess Augusta, including the great pagoda. (Yale Center for British Art, Paul Mellon Collection)

Below: Wealthy 'amateur' owners sometimes designed extraordinary landscape gardens. At Stourhead, Wiltshire, banker Henry Hoare designed a circuit walk around a lake, passing many buildings. This tribute to the Roman author Virgil in *The Aeneid* also evoked painter Claude's Arcadian coast view of Delos with Aeneas (see p. 18). (Yale Center for British Art, Paul Mellon Collection)

Henry Hoare at Stourhead, Wiltshire, and the Hon. William Hamilton, the relatively penurious younger son of an aristocrat, at Painshill, Surrey, who eventually ran out of money but left an amazing garden legacy. It is impossible to tell these designs from the hand of professionals. Both have been restored and are magical places to visit. Other owners often influenced professional designs. Lord Cobham at Stowe was a master at guiding his designers, employing Bridgeman, Kent and Brown – the three geniuses of their day – in pioneering schemes that were greatly admired. Lord Coventry guided Brown's work at Croome Court in his early days in the 1750s; Lord Scarsdale at Kedleston influenced William Emes' layout after architect Robert Adam left.

To turn the landscape garden into a work of art the simple palette of water, grass and trees, common to all great gardens, had to be applied expertly to the unique canvas in front of the designer. The formula had to be adapted to each individual site, so that no two gardens were the same. It also required other features to frame it and link everything together smoothly.

The house was always the hub. It had a strong visual and design relationship with its setting within and beyond the grounds, even though some parks were so large that the house seemed a remote feature in many parts. Sometimes it was built on a new site, or reused an older site where the house was demolished, or incorporated such as Croome Court in the 1750s. Or the existing building was left *in situ*, such as Vanbrugh's palace of the 1710s at Blenheim in the 1760s when Brown skilfully surrounded the palace with naturalistic grounds. Although Brown left some of Henry Wise's great formal avenues aligned on the house, there was no doubt that the British landscape style had vanquished the Frenchified formality Brown had otherwise swept away, much as the Duke of Marlborough had vanquished the French at the eponymous battle in 1704. Occasionally the pleasure grounds were not visible from the house, such as at Stourhead and Painshill, instead being remote havens of retreat in the Arcadian countryside that was so coveted.

The pleasure ground was the playground. It was generally kept close to the house for walks and dalliance, clothed in lush green lawns and floriferous shrubberies of native and new exotic plants. It was less intensively gardened than a flower garden and tended to be planted with shrubs in lawns, with meandering walks overlooking the park. To find one or two pleasure grounds of an acre or two, perhaps flanking the house, was common in modest designs. In the larger estates, such as Croome Court and Stowe, a series of pleasure grounds, in differing characters, might link around the park in a long and varied walk from the house, taking in the kitchen garden and views from garden buildings and the rolled gravel paths.

The country house was the hub of the landscape design. At Ickworth, Suffolk, a vast 1,800-acre park, pleasure ground and woodland surrounded the massive rotunda at the centre of the house. (S. Rutherford)

Above: Pleasure grounds were for pleasure! Walking, admiring views, listening to bird song, and gentle pastimes such as sketching or painting, with little buildings for tea parties and shelter in bad weather. Frogmore, Berkshire, in Windsor Home Park. (S. Rutherford)

Below: Ha-ha! The ha-ha at Chirk was used to fling open the view seamlessly from the pleasure ground over the park and beyond. Chirk Castle, Wrexham has a stone wall, but brick was also commonly used. (National Trust Photographic Library/Matthew Antrobus/Bridgeman Images)

Ah-ha! The ha-ha distinguished the true landscape garden by bursting open the views from the house and pleasure ground, far out over the park and way beyond, without an obvious break. Instead of an intrusive fence or wall to keep out unwanted animals, this surprise ditch and sunken wall invisibly divided the pleasure ground from the park, adapted from a military earthwork device first used in Europe. The livestock, deer and horses stayed safely at arm's length beyond the sunken retaining wall, giving the illusion that the park lawns came up to the house, and clear views of them radiated out from the house and pleasure ground. At many places, such as Petworth, the lawns really did come up to the house, so that Lord Egremont and his guests walked straight out of the austere mansion amongst the deer to Brown's distant lake (later so atmospherically painted by Turner). Even so, a ha-ha around the large Petworth pleasure ground to the side of the mansion ensured that the gravel walks were free of debris but enjoyed panoramic views of the park.

Did you know?

British Lawns were Renowned

Whatever the garden style, the British and Irish excelled at luxuriant emerald lawns, mainly because of the warm, damp climate. In the pleasure ground the lawn formed a smooth, calming, backcloth to the scene. The closely scythed turf was pleasant to walk on, moving from the verdant pleasure grounds to the more tussocky grazed sward of the park.

British lawns were the best and were highly prized. In gardens and pleasure grounds they were scythed and rolled to keep them short, like an emerald carpet. In the park they were grazed. (Bucks County Museum)

Thousands of garden buildings were built, for shelter, contemplation and socialising. Classical temples based on Greek or Roman models were a favourite, often dedicated to deities such as Bacchus, god of wine, or concepts such as Liberty. William Chambers' temple dedicated to William Shakespeare. (Yale Center for British Art, Paul Mellon Collection)

Moving through the landscape to drink in all the features and views in an ever-changing scene was important too. In the pleasure ground paths led the visitor on gentle walks between seats, sculptures and garden buildings, designed to take in the best views, and sometimes led to the nearby church. In the park, rides meandered through belts of trees and woodland in much the same way. A walk alongside or overlooking the lake was valued. The drives were not just to reach the house, but to show off as much of the extent and beautiful design of the grounds as possible, to convey the exquisite taste and wealth of the owner (even though he might have almost bankrupted himself with the cost of the works). Drives allowed the family and their visitors to come and go while taking in the beauty of as much as possible of the whole design. More direct access came with the service drives for the staff and lesser visitors, serving the stables, domestic offices and kitchen garden.

Ornamental park and garden buildings were essential throughout, and the more the better. The term 'folly' for these is a misnomer. Of the temples, bridges, boathouses, eye-catchers, hermitages, and many other sorts, most had a use as well as a decorative purpose. Styles burgeoned, including classical, Gothic, Chinese, Moorish, rustic and primitive. Certain models appear again and again. The three-arched bridge carrying the main drive or a road to the mansion was common, found at Chatsworth, Burghley, Compton Verney, Alnwick and Audley End. The rotunda was even more popular and appears in still more gardens and parks, based on the Temple of Vesta at Tivoli and then Vanbrugh's pioneering example at Stowe of around 1720. Columns shot up, based on Trajan's Column in Rome, together with obelisks based on ancient Egyptian models and, for the wealthiest, triumphal arches modelled on various antique Roman ones that the Grand Tourists had seen, often doubling as houses for estate staff. No collection of these ornamental structures was quite the same as any other and certainly each had a unique setting. Drives were guarded by a series of lodges at the gateways, sometimes very substantial, such as the screen by Adam at Syon Park, and Earl Temple's Corinthian Arch at Stowe.

Water was the most prized, but most expensive and least predictable, ingredient of the landscape garden. Britain did not naturally boast breath-taking sheets of water, except in the Lake District, which was inconveniently remote, and on the coast. Without being blessed with coastal or riverside positions such as Mount Edgcumbe, Devon, and Syon and Kew, twinned either side of the Thames near London, those who wanted to show off were forced to pay dearly to float their own prestigious lake by employing the latest water engineering technology, adapted from

The rotunda was a popular garden building, based on a Roman model at Tivoli. The first one was at Stowe, Bucks, by John Vanbrugh (c. 1719); this one is at nearby Wotton Underwood. (S. Rutherford)

land reclamation and drainage schemes in East Anglia. Generally the idea was to emulate a great river such as the rivers Arno in Florence, or classical Tiber in Rome, or the Thames, redolent of nationalistic mercantile wealth and colonial links. Even the 110-acre lake at Blenheim was called the Great River, though it was created out of the tiny tickle of the River Glyme by the doyen Brown.

The sheet of water was ideally placed in the middle ground of the views from the house, framed by the park and often the pleasure ground. The ends were disguised if possible in order to give the illusion of an endless river. Bridges carried drives across the water, to provide spectacular views, and sham bridges and cascades disguised dams.

Dams, sometimes 10 metres or more high, were major engineering triumphs, built of earth and rock-fill with clay cores and a clay blanket on the upstream face to waterproof. Brown built at least forty dams and was probably responsible for more than anyone else. Being robust, many survive today along with the lakes they support. However, leaks were common and if the landscaper was not skilled in gathering and channelling what were usually meagre water supplies, and ensuring they did not then escape, the owner was left with a boggy, smelly puddle that never worked. Luckily for the owners of Chatsworth, Derbyshire, the River Derwent obligingly ran through the park past the house and just needed tweaking by Brown and his men to make it tasteful. At Croome Court, Worcestershire, it took Brown much ingenuity and his men much sweat and toil in draining a morass to feed not just a new mile-long 'river' pretending to be the head of the Severn, but also an impressive lake too. The hand of man is blessedly invisible.

Trees were used in a few particular ways in endless different patterns: as scattered single specimens, in clumps framing or screening views, as blocks of screening woodland and in narrow belts sheltering the park. A small palette of species was based on woodland natives plus a few exotics. Oak, ash, sycamore and elm were staples. Others included European lime, London plane, sweet chestnut and beech, with evergreen Scots pine and cedars of Lebanon as punctuation marks year-round. Some places such as Petworth, Luton Hoo and Croome became renowned for their collections of newly introduced plants from North America and the Far East.

Above: The most prized part of the landscape was water as a river meandering past the house in the middle distance. Brown made a sinuous river-like lake from a tiny Chiltern seasonal bourne at Chalfont Park, Buckinghamshire. Thomas Girtin, c. 1796. (Yale Center for British Art, Paul Mellon Collection)

Below: Natural rivers made engineering easier, but still required work to make them fit into the park design. The River Derwent, Chatsworth, Derbyshire, was at the heart of Brown's design. (Chatsworth House Trust)

Above: European lime was a popular tree for its pale leaves and upright form, here in a grassy grove replanted in Horace Walpole's pleasure ground at Strawberry Hill, Middlesex. (Strawberry Hill Trust)
Below: The Cedar of Lebanon punctuated parks and pleasure grounds year-round, with characteristic evergreen layered branches. A trade-mark of Capability Brown, it was also planted in many other landscape gardens. (C. Gallagher)

In the pleasure ground trees were underplanted with shrubberies of evergreens and flowering shrubs. A small palette of evergreens included yew, box, holly, Portugal and cherry laurel and butcher's broom. Flowering shrubs included mock orange, lilac, roses and other plants that largely flowered in late spring and early summer. Scented types were valued. The trickle of foreign introductions that became a flood extended the flowering time and innovative autumn leaf colour.

Did you know?

Plants Flooded in From Abroad in the Eighteenth Century
The range of plants available before 1700 was limited, but the opening up of North America and other British colonies led to a flood of new flowering trees and shrubs including magnolias, camellias, kalmias, banksias and berberis. Many owners amassed large collections in their landscape gardens, including the 3rd Earl of Egremont at Petworth, the 3rd Earl of Bute at Luton Hoo and the 6th Earl of Coventry at Croome Court, Worcestershire. The Duchess of Beaufort had a botanic garden of exotics at Badminton.

Twisting pleasure ground lawns, framed by shrubberies of evergreens, flowers and trees, delighted the senses during a walk. Painshill Park, Surrey. (S. Rutherford)

Flowering shrubs newly introduced from North America brightened shrubberies, such as this kalmia. (S. Rutherford)

Shrubs were not planted in groups of one type. Rose, rock rose, Portugal laurel and yucca in an eighteenth-century scheme at Painshill, Surrey, form an unusual combination to our modern gardening eyes. (S. Rutherford)

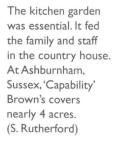

The kitchen garden was essential. It fed the family and staff in the country house. At Ashburnham, Sussex, 'Capability' Brown's covers nearly 4 acres. (S. Rutherford)

A large walled kitchen garden, sometimes covering several acres, was essential to the landscape garden, the larger the better, to impress. This walled Garden of Eden fed the family and household staff of the country house, and if near enough to London, the town house too. Ideally it lay at a distance, often out of sight of the house, when it came as a surprise destination on the pleasure ground walk, such as Harewood, Yorkshire; Ashburnham, Sussex, and Painshill, Surrey. Where an older landscape was remodelled, often the kitchen garden stayed put, next to the house as had been the previous convention. Surprisingly, at Croome the kitchen garden is quite close to the house, but is separated from it by Brown's large stable courtyard as an incident on the extensive pleasure ground circuit around the park. His kitchen garden at Wallington, Northumberland, is nearly half a mile distant from the house and formed a spectacular highlight at the furthest end of the pleasure ground walks.

Despite the serpentine line in the rest of the landscape garden, for practical reasons the layout of the kitchen garden paths and beds remained resolutely a grid pattern within geometric walls, and was probably enjoyed as a refreshing return to controlled geometry. As well as producing fruit and vegetables it was often used to grow the tender exotics of great rarity and value that were being introduced. Working glasshouses and ornamental conservatories were lavishly built.

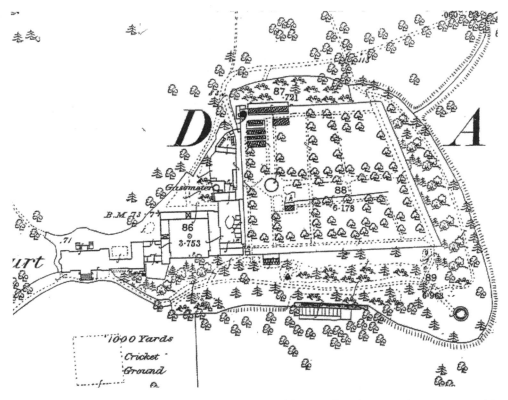

For practical reasons the kitchen garden kept rational lines and grid-pattern layout, screened by evergreens from the house (far left), or sited distantly in the park. At Croome Court, Worcestershire, Brown separated it from the house by a three-sided stable courtyard and surrounded it with a sinuous, narrow pleasure ground threaded through with a gravel walk taking in the view of the park from the rotunda (bottom right) above a ha-ha. (S. Rutherford)

The crinkle crankle wall is the extreme of garden walls: serpentine to make the most of the warming sun, sheltering fruit trees in the bays. (S. Rutherford)

When something is established there is a reaction and it starts to be lampooned. The landscape garden was no exception. Francis Coventry in *The World* in 1753 described how Squire Mushroom, a terrible social climber, by the age of forty had a considerable fortune. As well as clothes, a brace of whores and servants, he acquired a villa! It shot up into Gothic spires with battlements and contained numerous stuffed animals and swords and pistols. The triumph of his genius was in his gardens, containing everything in less than 2 acres: a yellow serpentine river, stagnating through a beautiful valley, nearly 20 yards long with a little ship with sails spread and streamers flying; a grove 'perplexed with errors and crooked walks'; an old hermitage, St Austin's Cave; and a temple to Venus where he 'riots with a couple of orange-wenches'.

Did you know?

Landscape Gardens to Visit
The list is endless, but the best of the best include Alnwick Castle, Northumberland; Harewood House, Yorkshire; Blenheim Palace, Oxfordshire; Chatsworth House, Derbyshire; Petworth House, Sussex; Berrington Hall, Herefordshire; Audley End, Essex; Prior Park, Bath; Longleat, Wiltshire; Wotton Underwood and West Wycombe, Buckinghamshire; and Strawberry Hill, Greater London.

5
Emotional Extremes: The Picturesque and Sublime, 1780s–1820s

By the 1770s and 1780s, reaction, inevitably, again set in. The offspring of the landscape garden were shaped by developing theories of emotional responses to visual stimuli, particularly by Burke in his *A Philosophical Enquiry into the Origin of Our Ideas of the Sublime and Beautiful* (1757), in which human instinct dictated reactions: the soft gentle curves of the beautiful appealed to male desires, while the sublime horrors appealed to desires for self-preservation. The style of the landscape garden began to be criticised

Gothic and Romantic sensibilities guided by philosophers such as the French author Rousseau led to a new appreciation of the Picturesque in landscape. *Philosopher in a Moonlit Churchyard*, de Loutherbourg, 1790. (Yale Center for British Art, Paul Mellon Collection)

as too bland, too smooth and formulaic. The design reaction, however, was still closely based on the established design formula of the landscape garden, and was labelled the Picturesque. Its still more frightening brother was the Sublime, imbued with an edgy sense of danger where possible by the dramatic scenery and use of paths and strategically placed and precipitous viewpoints to enhance this frisson of terror. These were part of the generation that revelled in Gothic tales of horror such as Horace Walpole's *Castle of Otranto* (1764) and William Beckford's *Vathek* (1786), alongside the powerful music of Beethoven and the impressionist paintings of Turner. Both those authors designed their landscape gardens, Beckford's Fonthill having a strong Picturesque feel. Later came Mary Shelley's very serious Gothic horror story *Frankenstein* (1818), along with Jane Austen's spoof Gothic novel *Northanger Abbey* (1817), and Thomas Rowlandson's satirical cartoons in *Dr Syntax's Tour in Search of the Picturesque*.

The Picturesque Style

The Picturesque was, together with the sublime and beautiful, the third element of a wider aesthetic movement. It was based on an appreciation of scenery and a range of prescribed

The unaltered natural landscape was now appreciated, the more dramatic the better. New designs used virgin natural features to make them more Picturesque, in the manner of a picture. Cresswell Crags is an enclosed limestone gorge, between Nottinghamshire and Derbyshire. George Stubbs, c. 1767. (Yale Center for British Art, Paul Mellon Collection)

emotions it provoked in the viewer. These terms were not easy to define, however, as they shifted seamlessly from one into the next. The word Picturesque was derived from 'painterly style', originating from paintings of Italian classical scenes by seventeenth-century artists including the three masters, Salvator Rosa, Poussin and Claude Lorrain. The range of emotions was codified, the terms such as beauty, horror, sublime and immensity, having specific meanings.

This style of architecture and landscaping used irregular, craggy and rugged forms and textures and asymmetrical layouts in attractive views in the later eighteenth century. The Picturesque was a less polished, rougher development of the landscape style, at its rugged best when the natural scenery was dramatic with a sense of wildness: irregular, varied and spectacular, such as in Wales and the Lake District. The planting was less well manicured and verged on the native.

The British Picturesque was defined by its chief arbiter the Revd William Gilpin in 1768, as 'expressive of that peculiar beauty which is agreeable in a picture'. His British guidebooks published between 1782 and 1809 helped to shift the emphasis of the term Picturesque from pictures to the landscape. A British equivalent of the European Grand Tour developed even before the Napoleonic Wars shut down European travel, with tourists descending upon the countryside, sketchbooks in hand, eager to experience this type of beauty and the emotions it aroused. Gilpin instructed visitors on the best viewpoints to seek (at particular 'stations'), and having made the effort, how to view these scenes formerly regarded with suspicion as unpleasant, wild and threatening, barren landscapes, and the emotions to be felt in particular places.

The ideal Picturesque landscape was dramatic, which was really only possible where the owner had hilly land to play with. Hot spots developed in the most vertiginous areas, in the Wye Valley, on the Welsh border, in the Lake District, mid-Wales, Devon, Derbyshire and Scotland where steep hillsides, cliffs, crags and rivers offered greater animation and an added dimension. The hand of man was even less obvious than in the

The River Wye on the Welsh/English border was one of a group of areas that were sought out by Picturesque tourists from the 1770s onwards, especially when Europe was inaccessible during the Napoleonic wars leading up to 1815. The ruins of Tintern Abbey were especially appreciated. Samuel Palmer, 1861. (Yale Center for British Art, Paul Mellon Collection)

Brownian landscape park. Dense woodland was planted on hillsides, broad tumbling rivers were embraced and enhanced with bathhouses, hermitages and other rustic and ruinous structures, and distant views of far-flung mountain ranges and eye-catchers, preferably ruined castles and abbeys, were framed beyond the estate. One result of the Picturesque was the appreciation and development of rock and quarry gardens.

In architecture, classical styles were rather too refined for the desired ruggedness. Influenced by the earlier landscapers and architects such as Sanderson Miller who used Gothic ruins as garden and park buildings, and Walpole's Strawberry Hill, Gothic came into its own in the Picturesque landscape. Various new houses resembled medieval abbeys and castles pretending to survive at the heart of ancient estates, redolent of forgotten civil wars and remote, suppressed religious houses.

The Picturesque Controversy, Payne-Knight and Price
In the later generation of the 1780s, two obscure gentlemen of the Welsh Borders, Richard Payne-Knight and Uvedale Price, seriously criticised Brown's designs as being without the visual and emotional interest of the rugged and sublime. They went into print in a bad-tempered argument with Humphry Repton. *Headlong Hall* (1816) alludes to Picturesque controversy, and Brown's landscape style as 'corrected – trimmed – polished'.

Sublime
Grand Tourists experienced a range of landscapes considered picturesque on the Continental journey. These included the terrors of the Alpine and Apennine passes and mountains, painted by Salvator Rosa. The tourists' reactions to the Alpine scenery changed as the century progressed and natural fear transformed into a positive liking for 'Salvator Rosa and Sublimity'. Travellers sought ever-wilder places and the writers of tourist guides responded to their new visual appetite. The reaction to the passage of the Alps gradually changed from a genuinely terrifying experience to one that induced awe and fear at the time, but which could be recalled at home with excitement and youthful pride at the dangers overcome.

The Sublime drew on the extreme dramatic end of the Picturesque emotional spectrum. Grand Tourists could scare themselves travelling across Alpine passes and then return home to try and recreate the frisson of terror in their own. *Landscape with Figures and Bridge*, J. M. W. Turner, n. d. (Yale Center for British Art, Paul Mellon Collection)

The Sublime

The Sublime was the scary extreme of the Picturesque landscape style. It was still more awe-inspiring, using the scale, wildness and natural ruggedness of a dramatic landscape to provoke feelings of dread or eternity. Hafod, Dyfed, a vast Welsh Sublime landscape, is still full of surprise and the frisson of danger and remoteness, along with Hawkstone, Shropshire, and Hackfall, North Yorkshire.

But the Picturesque and Sublime were a bit of a by-way in garden design. By the 1830s they had more or less died out as must-have fashions. The Picturesque lived on as a term coined to indicate the painterly use of the landscape in design but vanished as a style in its own right.

Did you know?

The Best Picturesque and Sublime Landscapes to Visit
Picturesque: Hestercombe, Somerset; Llanerchaeron, Ceredigion; Plas Newydd, Anglesey; Scotney Castle, East Sussex; Sheringham, Norfolk; Blaise Castle; and Hamlet, Bristol.
Sublime: Piercefield, Chepstow; Hackfall, Yorkshire; Hafod, Wales; Hawkstone, Shropshire.

Above left: A slippery, narrow path in a rocky gorge, with the thrill of the unknown at the end of it. Hawkstone Park, Shropshire. (Hawkstone Park Follies)

Above right: A brush with primitive emotions and feelings of danger epitomises the Sublime. Hafod's Cavern Cascade is invisible without braving an ominous hole in the rough rock. Clamber into a dark, wet, uneven tunnel, the thunderous sound of water increasing with every step, a turn into the dark reveals the pool, blinded by the light and deafened by the crashing water, the top of the cascade invisible. (Hafod Trust)

Right: The natural landform, used to brilliant effect in the vast Sublime landscape at Hafod. The Gothic Arcade recently restored above the tumultuous water. (Hafod Trust)

Above: Artificial and real ruins were important in Picturesque and Sublime landscapes. At Hawkstone, Shropshire, a 'ruined' arch is perched precariously at the top of a red sandstone cliff, framing a precipitous drop. (Hawkstone Park Follies)

Left: Dark caves and tunnels heighten the drama and the danger of the unknown in the Sublime landscape at Hawkstone to scare and exhilarate the visitor like a modern-day theme park. (Hawkstone Park Follies)

6

The Flower Garden Returns: Regency Gardening, 1790s–1820s

Much to the relief of everyone, by the 1800s the landscape designer Humphry Repton was spearheading the renaissance of the controlled and convenient flower garden around the house, banishing park lawns and anything more rugged to a civilised distance. This reinvention of the floral display as seen, smelt and easily reached from the house coincided with the 'Regency' period of the 1790s–1830s. This was most obvious in the garden terrace, which reappeared, separated from the landscape park and its inhabitants by a civilising terrace of stone or brick with a parapet or balustrade, or perhaps an ornamental fence. It clearly defined the difference between garden and park, entirely at odds with the invisible principle of the ha-ha. Often the flower garden overlooked a Picturesque park as the two were ideal companions, such as at Endsleigh, Devon (1814).

By 1800 a shift in the economy resulted in the social strata burgeoning below the politicians, squires, and aristocrats. The emerging merchant class required smaller houses

Formal flower terraces were allowed back next to the house in landscape designer Humphry Repton's designs. He designed Endsleigh for the Duke of Bedford around a new a country 'cottage' with an extensive Picturesque and floral landscape. (Hotel Endsleigh)

and estates, which reflected the taste and fashion of the day. Repton, although he acquired major aristocratic clients, benefitted considerably from the 'upstart wealth' as he classed it, the men who profited from war contracts and fund holding. The profits of Empire and slavery continued percolating through the whole British economy and funded the landscape aspirations of the Regency period.

Did you know?

Regency Landscape Designer Humphry Repton (1752–1818)
Repton was Brown's self-proclaimed successor, setting up in 1788, five years after the Master's death. His ambition was to become the most well-known and prolific landscape designer. He set out to design in the landscape style, but later in his career he re-introduced the flower garden and terraces around the house, instead of park lawns and livestock up to the windows. Unlike Brown he was a great self-publicist and published his advice and theories. His clients received his advice in beguiling Red Books (so-called because they were bound in red morocco leather), containing attractive watercolour paintings, using lift-up flaps to show the scenery before and after his proposals. His most complex commissions included Woburn Abbey, Bedfordshire; Ashridge, Hertfordshire; Attingham Park, Shropshire; Endsleigh, Devon; and Kenwood, London.

Landscape designer Humphry Repton (1752–1818) began to reinstate the flower garden around the house. His trade card shows him as a gentleman, surveying, with a team of labourers and foreman to do the hard work. (M. Thompson)

Regency villas sprang up, smaller than country houses, miniaturising the landscape garden, with elegant conservatories, mini-lakes and flower gardens. A villa and garden painted by George Shepheard, c. 1820. (Yale Center for British Art, Paul Mellon Collection)

This new class of smaller properties, including merchants' villas, was often sited at the edge of growing towns and cities, and the owners had to cope with the cost of living in the Napoleonic Wars and higher taxes. So for these owners, for reasons of space and finance, a great park was not an option. A divide emerged between landscaping and gardening. The garden became an attainable frame for the wider landscape, both within the owner's property and beyond in the 'borrowed' landscape. The sweeping landscape park was for the super-rich and in these smaller estates it could only be suggested. So a paddock of several acres, with one or two milch cows, evoked the park, making 'dressed' grounds immediately around the house essential, with flowering shrubberies in lawns, flower beds to display the greater range of plants available, trellises, and ornate garden seats.

The more elegant grounds complemented the lighter playfulness of the architecture that was developing by 1800 in the hands of architects such as John Soane and John Nash, which was ideally suited to smaller-scale villa residences of taste. Nash and Repton and their contemporaries regarded buildings and their landscape as 'a picturesque whole'. The graceful smaller houses in pared-down classical style more easily straddled the divide between the house and grounds, using French windows opening onto verandahs with striped canopies, and balconies, conservatories and flower corridors and then into the flowering shrubbery. The wider availability of ornamental ironwork enabled these confections to be built, as well as sweeping curvilinear glasshouses for new tender plants.

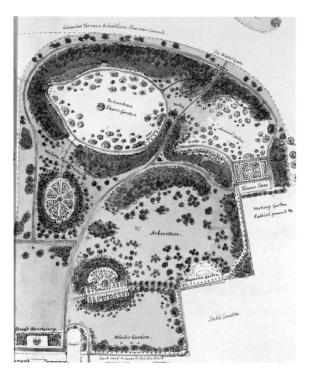

Left: Repton excelled himself at Ashridge, Bucks, in 1813. It was a child of his old age. Many varied flower gardens in lawns were linked by paths around the vast new Gothic 'abbey' mansion. (Getty Research Institute, Los Angeles)

Below: The Flower Garden, one of the gardens scattered in Repton's 'Modern Garden' at Ashridge (Red Book 1813). Painted trellis with arches and obelisks framed the garden and many little flower beds studded the lawn. (Getty Research Institute, Los Angeles)

Did you know?

Jane Austen and Regency Gardening
This was the world of the fashionable Regency milieu who congregated in London, Brighton and Bath, and of course of Jane Austen who poked gentle fun at Repton in *Mansfield Park*. The nouveau riche Mr Rushworth wanted to improve his country estate. '"Your best friend upon such an occasion," said Miss Bertram calmly, "would be Mr. Repton, I imagine." "That is what I was thinking of. As he has done so well by Smith, I think I had better have him at once. His terms are five guineas a day."'

Now it was rehabilitated, the garden needed a variety of scenes, the more the better, to impress. This was provided in a selection of themed areas, some of which might make a return to a geometric layout of the Stuarts and the French, or be in a lax floral and shrubbery scatter in lawns. Repton's Red Book designs for Woburn Abbey, Bedfordshire, and Ashridge, Hertfordshire, show much inventiveness and variety in quite sizeable gardens. At Ashridge (1813), a child of his old age along with Woburn, he suggested over a dozen areas scattered within the lawns and linked by paths, including a Monks' Garden (imitating a floral burial ground), an underground grotto tunnel called a Souterrein, several flower gardens including for annuals and roses, a winter garden and an arboretum.

In a park at Old Warden, Bedfordshire, the cult of the Swiss picturesque put in the most convincing appearance in gardening in the 1820s as the Swiss Garden. A series of linked scenes was created in ten acres supposedly evoking an Alpine theme. A rustic Swiss chalet

Repton's Rose Garden, Ashridge (1813), replanted with old-fashioned roses. The stone pillars and swags that surrounded it (instead of the suggested trellis) have gone. (C. Beddall)

Repton's Children's Garden, Endsleigh (1814). Geometric flower beds below a sheltering loggia reached from the house overlook the River Tamar winding Picturesquely in the valley far below. (S. Rutherford)

at the heart was surrounded by endless ornate little iron bridges over the wriggling 'rivers', with a labyrinthine grotto, a kiosk, shrubbery walks, seats and many urns and other sculpture. Rustic unpeeled bark and pine cone decorations help to add the Swissery. This was all ground-breaking design and heralded the Gardenesque and Victorian gardening of the later century when as many different plant displays as possible were required in gardens of all sizes.

Regency Shrubberies

A new and distinctive feature in the pleasure ground was the Regency ornamental shrubbery, and the main guide to planting was Henry Phillips' *Sylva Florifera* (1823). These varied shrubberies framed the sinuous walks in less formal parts of the pleasure ground, combining flowers, shrubs and trees in a more naturally grouped manner, so that they were closely connected with the landscape. J. C. Loudon in 1804 summed up what Regency gardening aimed to do in using the variety of trees, shrubs and flowers by providing a succession of perpetual interest all year round, particularly in summer, something gardeners still strive to do today.

The key to the new shrubbery was yet more irregularity, in using plants in groups and thickets of various sizes, 'gliding into one another on smooth lawn, beautifully varied, broken into small scenes by trees and shrubs of the most elegant sorts'. All this was linked by smooth gravel walks winding in a 'graceful, easy manner'. The innovation was, instead of growing single specimens, to mass the different sorts in groups to make a stronger display of each, a principle that still guides gardeners today. Colour clashes were encouraged. Phillips recommended one particular combination of purple lilac and yellow laburnum. Against a spine of evergreens and a few trees, surrounded by the flowering shrubs, tall spiry herbaceous plants and annuals punctuated the gaps before the shrubs grew in and suppressed them, including hollyhocks, lilies, sunflowers, foxgloves and Jacob's ladder. The beds were enclosed by bands and pockets of lower herbaceous plants such as geraniums, paeonies and bulbs, which bled into the surrounding grass. Evergreens included laurel, box, holly and phillyrea, many of which seem commonplace to us now. Popular flowering shrubs included dogwoods, viburnum, lilacs, Philadelphus, roses, kalmia, brooms and gorse.

The Royal Pavilion, Brighton

The most famous of these Regency villas was the Prince Regent's Royal Pavilion at Brighton, his marine residence which exemplified the cult of the exotic. From a reserved classical villa, it mushroomed into an exotic fantasy of Indian and the oriental by John Nash for his extravagant client, with domes sprouting madly, 'as if St Paul's Cathedral has come down to Brighton and pupped', so Sydney Smith said. In a modest and highly public garden in the heart of the newly fashionable town, lawns and shrubberies were arranged in the new rather shaggy Regency style. Repton was unhappily ousted from designing the grounds by Nash, but his far more inventive proposals to provide a 'true garden' with 'rich embellishments' had included an Indian pool with an island for musicians, a long conservatory corridor for flower and fragrance, and an oriental-style aviary like a sky rocket.

The landscape park, amended with Reptonian flower gardens, was enthusiastically embraced by the Victorians, who used it as the framework for private country estates, for public parks and even lunatic asylums. Royalty continued to make it fashionable for country houses, when Queen Victoria and Prince Albert built their country retreats at Osborne House on the Isle of Wight and Balmoral in Scotland. Industrialists and newspaper barons surrounded their vast Victorian piles with them as did William Armstrong at Cragside in Northumberland, and *Times*

The Royal Pavilion, Brighton, was a masterpiece in Regency planting, with both stud flower beds and drifting shrub beds in lawn. John Nash, 1826. (Bridgeman Images)

editor John Walter at Bearwood in Berkshire. The most impressive group was for the banking Rothschilds in and around Buckinghamshire, including Waddesdon Manor, Mentmore Towers, Halton House, and Gunnersbury Park, Ealing. New types of landscapes adapted the style, including the public park in places such as Victoria and Battersea Parks, London, and many in the new industrial cities in Britain and the Empire. Even the hundred or more Victorian lunatic asylums were modelled on the secluded country house set in its extensive Brownian landscape park, to help cure the patients with cheering grounds and vistas.

Did you know?

The Best Regency Gardens to Visit
Ashridge, Hertfordshire; The Swiss Garden and Woburn Abbey, Bedfordshire; The Royal Pavilion, Brighton; Attingham, Shropshire; Endsleigh Hotel, Devon.
   Waddesdon Manor, Bucks, is a superb late landscape park with formal flower gardens that developed in the Victorian period (1837–1901) after the Regency.

The Indian style appeared in Regency gardens, most lavishly at Sezincote, Gloucestershire, in the 1820s. (Trevor Morris)

7
What Now?

Further reading
Make the most of the experience of visiting landscape gardens by doing a bit of further reading. This provides more of a feel for the Georgian world, which had such an effect on promoting the style, and is itself an exciting and sometimes racy period. Guide books are a great start, but these titles will give you a wider picture, greater detail and more about that Georgian background that spawned such great works of art.

Bapasola, Jeri, *The Finest View in England: The Landscape and Gardens at Blenheim Palace* (Blenheim Palace, 2009).
Daniels, Stephen, *Humphry Repton* (Yale, 1999).
Laird, Mark, *The Flowering of the Landscape Garden* (Penn, 1999).
Mowl, Tim, *Gentlemen and Players: Gardeners of the English Landscape* (Sutton, 2000).
Richardson, Tim, *The Arcadian Friends* (Bantam, 2007).
Rutherford, Sarah, *Capability Brown and his Landscape Gardens* (National Trust, 2016).
Rutherford, Sarah and Lovie, Jonathan, *Georgian Garden Buildings* (Shire, 2012).
Williamson, Tom, *Polite Landscapes: Gardens and Society in Eighteenth-Century England* (Tempus, 1995).

Web resources
The internet brings us a previously unimaginable variety of resources for finding out more about individual landscape gardens or the style as a whole.

Parks & Gardens UK is the leading online resource for historic parks and gardens.
www.parksandgardens.org/

Garden Finder database
www.gardenvisit.com/gardens

Yale Centre for British Art has many historic images of the Landscape Garden.
britishart.yale.edu/collections/search

The website of the CB300 Festival celebrating Capability Brown and the English Landscape
http://www.capabilitybrown.org

Humphry Repton Red Books online; play with sliders he used to show 'before' and 'after' scenes.
http://dxlab.sl.nsw.gov.au/repton-flip-book-2/

Repton's colourful Rose Garden design, Ashridge, Bucks (1813), with swags, trellis and a central fountain. It was not built in quite this way. (Getty Research Institute, Los Angeles)

Places to Visit

The only way to understand the unique artistry of the landscape garden is by visiting and appreciating for yourself the 'genius of the place' and the talent of the designer in using it. The subtlety of the 'natural' but in fact man-made appearance can only be picked out when you visit and take time to walk round and try and guess what is the hand of man. The more places you visit, the more of a picture you can build up. Try and pick out just how cleverly each was put together using the local conditions of topography, climate and soils, and applying the landscape garden formula: water, grass and trees with drives, views, garden buildings, pleasure ground and kitchen garden. Compare them and see for yourself their similarities and differences. Some incorporate earlier formal garden features such as parterres, straight canals and avenues; others have been added to since they were laid out, but usually this has not destroyed the Georgian landscaper's vision. Many landscape gardens are open to the public including the following:

Antony House, Torpoint, Cornwall www.nationaltrust.org.uk/main/w-antony (Picturesque, Repton)

Ashridge, Berkhamsted, Hertfordshire Garden: ashridge.org.uk/about-us Park: www.nationaltrust.org.uk/ashridge-estate (Brown park, Repton gardens)

Audley End www.english-heritage.org.uk/visit/places/audley-end-house-and-gardens/ (Brown)

Attingham www.nationaltrust.org.uk/attingham-park (Picturesque, Repton)

Blenheim Palace, Oxfordshire www.blenheimpalace.com (Brown's masterpiece, a World Heritage Site)

Boughton House, Northamptonshire http://www.boughtonhouse.co.uk/ (the English Versailles)

Bramham Park, Yorkshire www.bramhampark.co.uk (formal French-style gardens)

Castle Howard, North Yorkshire www.castlehoward.co.uk (formal garden and avenues)

Chatsworth House, Derbyshire www.chatsworth.org (London and Wise formality in the garden with Brown landscape park)

Chiswick House, Greater London www.chgt.org.uk (Kent's work with his patron Lord Burlington)

Cirencester Park, Gloucestershire www.cirencesterpark.co.uk (formal French pleasure ground)

Compton Verney, Warwickshire www.comptonverney.org.uk (Brown)

Croome Court, Worcestershire www.nationaltrust.org.uk/croomepark (masterpiece by Brown)

Endsleigh Hotel, Milton Abbot, Tavistock, Devon http://hotelendsleigh.com (Picturesque and Repton flower garden)

Gibside, Tyne & Wear beta.nationaltrust.org.uk/home/item248903 (landscape park)

Hackfall, North Yorkshire www.hackfall.org.uk (Sublime)

Hagley Hall, West Midlands www.hagleyhall.com (landscape park)

Hampton Court Palace, Middlesex http://www.hrp.org.uk/hampton-court-palace/#gs .LawLEFM (formal French and Dutch gardens)

Hawkstone, Shropshire www.principal-hayley.com/venues–hotels/hawkstone-park.aspx (Sublime)

Hestercombe, Somerset hestercombe.com (Picturesque)

Kedleston Hall, Derbyshire www.nationaltrust.org.uk/main/w-kedlestonhall (landscape garden and park)

Kenwood House, London www.english-heritage.org.uk/visit/places/kenwood (Repton)

Melbourne Hall www.melbournehall.com/ (formal French-style garden)

Mount Edgcumbe, Cornwall www.mountedgcumbe.gov.uk (landscape garden)

Painshill, Surrey www.painshill.co.uk (landscape garden by amateur owner)

Painswick Rococo Garden, Gloucestershire www.rococogarden.co.uk (Rococo)

Petworth House, West Sussex www.nationaltrust.org.uk/petworth-house-and-park

Prior Park, Bath www.nationaltrust.org.uk/priorpark/ (Brown)

Rousham, Oxfordshire www.rousham.org (a masterpiece by Kent, adapting a Bridgeman layout)

Royal Botanic Gardens, Kew, London www.kew.org (two great landscape gardens, one by Brown, joined together as a botanic garden)

Royal Pavilion, Brighton brightonmuseums.org.uk/royalpavilion (Regency garden)

Saltram, Plymouth, Devon www.nationaltrust.org.uk/saltram (landscape garden)

Scotney Castle, East Sussex www.nationaltrust.org.uk/scotney-castle (Picturesque)

Sezincote, Moreton-in-Marsh, Gloucestershire http://www.sezincote.co.uk (Reptonian with Indian decoration)

Shugborough, Staffordshire www.shugborough.org.uk (landscape garden)

Stourhead, Somerset www.nationaltrust.org.uk/stourhead (landscape garden by amateur owner)

Stowe, Buckinghamshire www.stowe.co.uk, www.nationaltrust.org.uk/stowe (the greatest landscape garden with work by designers Bridgeman, Kent and Brown)

Strawberry Hill, Greater London www.strawberryhillhouse.org.uk (Rococo by an influential owner)

Studley Royal, North Yorkshire beta.nationaltrust.org.ukfountains-abbey (formal French-style water garden, Picturesque surroundings, a World Heritage Site)

Syon Park, Greater London www.syonpark.co.uk/ (Brown)

The Swiss Garden, Old Warden, Bedfordshire http://www.shuttleworth.org/swissgarden/ 'A miniature world, dotted with follies as absurdly pretty as illustrations in a fairy tale.'

The Swiss Cottage, Endsleigh, Devon, a rustic cottage orné, is a feature in a remote part of Repton's Picturesque design, far out in the grounds, overlooking the Tamar valley. (Hotel Endsleigh)

Westbury Court, Gloucestershire www.nationaltrust.org.uk/westbury-court-garden (formal Dutch garden)

Wentworth Castle, South Yorkshire www.wentworthcastle.org (landscape garden and park)

West Wycombe Park, Buckinghamshire www.nationaltrust.org.uk/main/w-westwycombepark (landscape garden and park)

Wimpole Hall, Cambridgeshire www.wimpole.org (formal avenues; later landscape by Brown)

Woburn Abbey, Bedfordshire www.woburn.co.uk (Repton gardens)

Wrest Park, Bedfordshire www.english-heritage.org.uk/daysout/properties/wrest-park (French style, later work by Brown)

Wales

Clytha Castle, Abergavenny www.landmarktrust.org.uk (occasional open days) (Picturesque)

Hafod, Ceredigion, www.hafod.org (Sublime)

Llanerchaeron, Aberaeron, Dyfed www.nationaltrust.org.uk/llanerchaeron (Picturesque)

Newtown House (Dinefwr), Llandeilo www.nationaltrust.org.uk/dinefwr (landscape park, work by Brown)

Piercefield, Chepstow www.wyevalleyaonb.org.uk/images/uploads/general/Picturesque_ Piercefield.pdf (Sublime)

Plas Newydd, Anglesey www.nationaltrust.org.uk/plas-newydd-country-house-and-gardens (Picturesque and Repton)

The Kymin, Monmouth www.nationaltrust.or.uk/main/w-thekymin-2 (Picturesque)

Tredegar House, Newport www.nationaltrust.org.uk/tredegar-house

Scotland

Blair Castle, Perthshire www.blair-castle.co.uk (formal garden)

Chatelherault and Strathclyde Country Parks, Hamilton, Lanarkshire (the former High and Low Parks associated with Hamilton Palace) www.visitlanarkshire.com

Tredegar.

A major labour force had to make the landscape garden, shifting enormous quantities of earth and rocks by hand. Tredegar House, South Wales, the grounds designed by Adam Mickle.

Culzean Castle, Ayrshire www.nts.org.uk/property/culzean-castle-country-park
Ossian's Cave and Hall at The Hermitage, Dunkeld, Scotland www.nts.org.uk/property/
    Hermitage (Picturesque/sublime)
Stirling Castle www.stirlingcastle.gov.uk (formal)

Getting Involved
The Gardens Trust promotes the study of garden history and is the umbrella organisation for local County Gardens Trusts:
thegardenstrust.org

Look for your local County Gardens Trust at:
http://thegardenstrust.org/conservation/find-local-cgts/
The National Trust provides varied opportunities to volunteer in historic gardens countrywide in many ways:
www.nationaltrust.org.uk/volunteer

The Georgian Group is the national charity dedicated to preserving Georgian buildings and gardens:
https://georgiangroup.org.uk/

Kent's hedged exedra at Chiswick in south-west London. This is the dark backdrop to a collection of white classical statues, seen along a lawned vista from Lord Burlington's famous Italianate villa. (Chiswick House Gardens, photo by Richard Bryant)

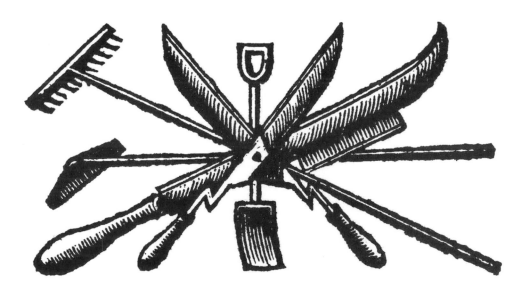